The
Freedom
Of The Will

By

Early
Free Will Baptists
Ministers

FWB
FWB Publications
Columbus, Ohio

INTRODUCTION

Two of the earliest Free Baptist ministers and writers that wrote on the subject of the Freedom of the Will were Enoch Mack, M.D. and Dr. Ransom Dunn.

Mack in 1833 signed the Declaration of Sentiments put forth by the anti-society movement and became attracted to the Free Baptists because of their anti-slavery sentiments and became an early contributor to the *Morning Star.* In 1835 William Burr suggested he move to Dover, New Hampshire where he became the pastor of the First Free Will church. He later became the Corresponding Secretary of the Foreign and Home Mission Societies but still was an editorial contributor of the *Morning Star.*

Dunn, was also an early pastor in Dover at the Washington Ave. Free Baptist Church which still remains today as the Dover Baptist Church. He was known for his leadership as an educator at Rio Grande College and Geauga Seminary both in Ohio and Hillsdale College in Michigan. He was an excellent speaker and notable writer.

Both contributed to the Freedom of the Will in this book as separate writings.

Freedom Of The Will

FREEDOM OF THE WILL

BY
ENOCH   MACH

FREEDOM is a prominent quality of the human mind.-If, among the attributes with which the Creator has invested the soul, there is one preeminently ennobling and god-like, it is, freedom to will', and freedom to perform what it wills. 'Without this, man, with the possession of all other faculties. Were a machine: with it, he is MAN. Destitute of this, all the other properties of his mind, and all the faculties of his body, would be controlled by external.

Influence by a power, or by powers out of himself: Possessed   of   this   attribute,   the controlling power is in himself. Unblest with freedom of the will, all the faculties of the understanding, and all the emotions, or affections and passions of the soul, would be the sport of external attractions or Repulsions, subject to the absolute dictation of fortuitous motive, or the absolute power of superior intelligence; or to the mutually conflicting and oppressive influences of their own warring, unbalanced powers: while the corporeal faculties would be at the mercy of both dangerous influences without,. And of reigning, warring, uncontrolled passions within. But, endowed, as the soul is, with a free will, it stands erect amidst the intellectual and moral, and the physical and corporeal universe; ERECT, in the image of its Creator; free to WILL, free to ACT-limited, however, to a sphere assigned it by that Power who reserves to himself the prerogative of Raying to all other power!!, 'hitherto mayest thou come: and here shalt thou be stayed!' Man, erect, in the midst of a universe populous with intellectual beings and corporeal formations, by his bodily senses and the faculties of his understanding, contemplates his condition, the blessings arid evil!! that surround him, the motive that address him, and the authorities which command him; and by this faculty, freedom of the will, he yields to or resists attractive and repulsive influences and motives; chooses or refuses proffered objects and suggested courses of conduct; and obeys or disobeys the laws of his Maker: A self-controlling agent, subjecting his desires and passions to reason and the Jaws of god; or yielding himself, the whole soul, the whole man, to the sway of his appetites and passions, and to the influences of temptation.

This doctrines well attested by Adam, if Milton be allowed to speak for' him, while yet standing in his integrity; his understanding unbeclouded by sin, and his judgment and testimony unwarped by guilt: ----Best are all things as the will Of God ordained them: His creating hand nothing imperfect or deficient left Of all that be created; - much less man, Or aught that might his happy state secure, Secure from outward force; within himself The danger lie , *yet lie within his power:·* Against his WILL he-can receive no harm.

But God LEFT FREE THE WILL; for what obeys Reason, is *free;* and Reason he made right, But bid her well beware, and still erect; Lest, by some fair-appearing good surprised, she dictate false; and misinform the WILL to do what God expressly bath forbid.
Paradise Lost, Book IX.

But, among mankind, the existence of this faculty-this attribute of the human soul, so prominent, so preeminent, so ennobling, so god-like-is doubted, disbelieved, denied, and disputed! What! Has man become so ignorant of himself! And to himself so great a traitor, as to disclaim that high attribute bestowed by his Creator, constituting him, more than any other, his Maker's image! Will man thus libel his Creator to disinherit himself of what mostly makes him man! To make himself a poor machine! How has this come to pass 1 Man, in losing the necessary knowledge of his Maker, has lost the needful knowledge of himself. In that same light by which he sees his God, he sees himself: and that darkness which conceals from his view the character and attributes of his God, conceals from his sight his own attributes and' character. And, as with the loss of a knowledge of God, he loses a knowledge of himself; so, with the recovery of the knowledge of his Maker, he recovers a knowledge of himself.

Hence, the freedom of the will is most sternly denied and obstinately disputed, where the ••darkness covering the people, "in respect to life character and attributes of God, is most "gross." And hence, in enlightened, Christian communities, those individuals who have most sinned against spiritual light, and plunged themselves into deep darkness, far from God and beyond the light of his Spirit, are ready to attribute their character and conduct and destiny, to a resistless fatality; denying the freedom of the human will for resisting what they call the laws of necessity.

Let us approach that poor Hindoo, prostrate in adoration before a god which his own or other human hands have fashioned into what he regards as a divinity.

Let us admonish him; and teach him of his sinfulness. He acknowledges himself to be a sinner. But he justifies himself in his sins. He pleads fatality and the decrees of the gods. He declares he could not possibly be otherwise than as he it. If we may put into his mouth an argument actually employed by a Hindoo in reply to the admonitions of one of the English General Baptist missionaries, he argues justification of his wickedness by comparing himself, in his alleged inability to do otherwise than his fate determines, to the inability of a tree to produce fruit differing from its natural kind. "If," says he, "you plant a mango tree, will it not produce mangoes 7"Yes. "Well then, I am created a sinner; how can I do otherwise than sin? "

A consideration of the laws of the human mind, and the nature of the human heart, will discover to us the origin and progress of these dark and deadly waters--the doctrine of man's unavoidable passive- ness in the formation of his character, in his conduct; and in the de- termination of his destiny.

By due exercise of any one of the powers or faculties of the soul, that power or faculty maintains its proper influence among the others, and acquires increased strength; and in proportion as it is exercised in opposition to the others, or to their neglect, it rises to an ascendency over them. Contemplate man in that state of uprightness to which he was created. The will sits enthroned over the other faculties of the soul, the understanding and the affections and emotions, and over the corporeal appetites. It is fully competent to control and balance the whole, in complete conformity to the laws given us by our Maker. Man's faithful exercise of this will, would preserve its original ascendency. But he does not faithfully exercise it. He perverts it to the favor of unholy temptation, or yields up its power to the influence of passion and appetite that moment he is a fallen being. His faculties are. lamentably marred. The balancing power has yielded its scepter, or become shorn of a portion of its strength. To-passion and appetite it has yielded at least a11art of its throne. The power of these passions and appetites becomes increased, proportionally as the power of the will is resigned, and as it wanes. For a while, "to will may be present with him;" but "how to perform, he finds not. "He has yielded his strength to the captivity of sin. The appetites and passions become stronger and stronger by repeated indulgence, until the will is utterly dethroned, bound in the chains of sinful propensity, or won over, degraded to subservience, to the dictates of passion and appetite. He is conscious, in some measure, of his degradation and wickedness. But his heart is too proud, wickeder darkened, to acknowledge that *he* is to be blamed for this, or that he has brought himself to this condition. He attempts to throw the blame on some other; at first, perhaps, like Adam after his transgression, upon a fellow creature; then, perhaps, like Eve, upon the serpent. He will sooner deny his attribute of freedom of the will, than own his guilt. He would fain make himself a mere machine, rather than be a free soul and therefore guilty in the ligation of his Maker's law and his neighbor's rights. Yea, sooner will he plead himself the passive instrument of Satan, than acknowledge himself so wicked as to have become voluntarily his servant. He would rather profess 'himself mere machine moved by the weakest and wildest influence, or a passive tool even of 'Satan; than to concede! Himself guilty, as he must by allowing the freedom of his will.

But as he progresses in sin he becomes more darkened, and more; Impious still; and in his darkness and his pride, spurning the imputation of passive subservience to Satan or his renown creature, as when as denying his own moral freedom, he casts the imputation on a non-descript power, that great something-nothing, which he calls Fate; Or are proud and impious still, he throws 'the whole responsibility and blame upon hill Maker, either indirectly, by making him to be the author of imperious fate, or directly, by attributing his character and his sins to the specific and irrevocable decrees of the Holy One, whom be avers has fixed all things as they occur, by a resistless necessity.

Human nature can arrive at no greater height of ingenuity in excusing itself from guilt and in sparing its pride, than by charging its sins and crimes to God; although in this case it denies its own noblest attribute, freedom to will and act, and avows itself machine, a mere tool. But what height of impiety to attribute to God, the power that moves such a machine and employs such a tool for working wickedness! Professing themselves as wise as this, they become fools indeed. Their foolish hearts are darkened-and they are given up to believe the lives of their own and Satan's invention. They are sold under sin. They are led captive by Satan at *his will*-for they have voluntarily surrendered *their* will to his chains. And the climax of their captivity is, the dreadful delusion that God is the Author of their sins, that he is such a one as themselves, having pleasure in iniquity, and that his will and resistless power, rather than their own choice and Satan's power, has made them what they are, and moves them as they are moved! How self-deluding!

How reproachful to the Holy One!

In this condition, that Redemption which appears from heaven, in the person of our Lord Jesus Christ, finds our lost souls! He comes to open our blinded eyes, that we may see our own character, and the character of our God-to unseal our ears, that we may hear the commands, instructions, invitations, warnings and threatening's uttered by him who cannot lie-to open the prison doors and rend asunder the chains wherein our souls are bound by Satan-to raise up the sub- verted, captivated WILL, proffering the aid of his arm Omnipotent to replace it upon the throne of the soul, and re-invest it with the scepter over the passions and appetites-to present before our revolted, perverted affections, the mighty motive of Heaven's bleeding love towards us sinners, exciting us to turn from Satan unto God, to hate our sins that made him bleed, and to revolt from their cruel dominion-and he came to show us through faith's glass, a world of glory be- yond the grave, to which he will raise all those who believe in him unto obedience of his gospel; a kingdom where they who will be righteous aha!! Shine forth as the brightness of the sun forever and ever; and eternal life in glory, to be rendered to those who will seek for glory, honor, and immortality in him: While, on the other hand, he shows the condemnation of the unrepentant, unbelieving-a life of darkness-a resurrection to damnation-and a judgment to ever- lasting fire 'Prepared for the devil and his angels!

In all this merciful and mighty interposition, he leaves the WILL to yet be FREE as he created it at first.   He puts forth his saving hand to it: but it is to save it *free.*

He *helps it*: but lays not compulsive force upon it.   That freedom which he originally gave it, is preserved in sacredness, in all his dealings with it. When it asks the helping of his mighty hand, to aid it in breaking the chains in which Satan has bound it, and to regain its ascendancy over passions, appetites and habits by which it has suffered itself to be overcome,-the aid implored is in mercy given. Strongest motives are presented-Means of grace are afforded-instructions are given-and the Holy Spirit 'said is offered-and still he leaves free the human will;- free to come to him ; free to refuse the life he offers ; and still free, after the soul has come, to continue to abide in him and follow him onward quite to death and glory; or to abide not in him, to go back and .food no more after him, to turn from the commandment once received, to become entangled again in the power of sin and wiles of Satan, and to turn back again to perdition.

The truth of Jesus, when accepted, "maketh free indeed. "His law is well declared to be the perfect law of liberty."

It is compatible with the utmost freedom of the will- yea, it re- quires the utmost freedom of the will to make its fulfillment possible-while the follower of Jesus conflicts with temptation, the powers of darkness, and the ills of life, in his militant course through this world. That same freedom will remain an attribute of his soul when it shall arise to join in the services and joys of heaven. It will exist as an attribute 'Of his soul forever. He will be MAN eternally!-man once lost-man regenerate-man redeemed-man glorified-but never man *unmade!* Never divested of one of those attributes conferred upon him in his creation. To destroy the works of Satan our Savior came: not to destroy his own!

If, as we have observed, the freedom of the mind is extensively-denied in theory and in the heart darkened by sin and swayed by pride; it is *universally* acknowledged in the conscience and in the practice of mankind: All law for the regulation of human conduct, is a recognition of the soul's freedom to will and to act as it wills.- Ail precepts, penalties and rewards derive their sanction from this principle.

And where exists, where has ever existed, a people altogether destitute of law for the regulation of society and the direction and restraint of individual conduct!

Whatever fabulous accounts may have been, or may be invented, of men attached immovably 'to rock, as polupi, the lowest species of animalization; or growing fast in the soil, rooted to one spo t like a plant; we cannot stretch our credulity to the belief that anybody of people have ever existed, or ever will exist, without some rules, with penalties and rewards, for the regulation of the community, the family, or the individual. And yet, all enactment of law; and all acknowledgement 'Of law; how rude or immature so ever the law may be, whether it be written on statute books of the state, or promulgated in oral decrees of the emperor, king, governor, magistrate1 chief, parent, or any undividable; or whether it be merely understood-all such enactment, and all such acknowledgement, is made upon the principle, fully recognized and conceded, that man's will is free to will, and his whole intellect free to act as his own will dictates.

There obtains also, a universal sense of Right and Wrong. No people so lost to humanity as to have no sense of virtue and vice: -none but attach the idea of right to some acts, and of wrong to others. This sense has its existence in the sentiment of man's freedom-of will. And the sentiment that whatever is regarded as virtuous, should be commended and rewarded in the individual that practices it; and that whatever is regarded as vicious is to be disapproved, censured, and punished-in him that does it-is a sentiment which obtains universally. Though this sentiment may be, in some communities' mild, in some individuals exceedingly weak and quite perverted, yet the sentiment is universally felt and manifest, and is a universal acknowledgement that the human mind is free to will and to act. And where is the fatalist, so completely a fatalist, as not to habitually betray the falsity of his theory and the error of his heart.

This he does by his recognition of right and wrong in his neighbor's actions; by manifest approbation of what he regards as virtue and censure of what he regards as vice. Still farther than this, he recognizes the freedom of the soul to form and control its own sentiments, as well as to dictate and restrain outward actions. This he does by mani-fest and expressed condemnation or censure of those whose sentiments differ from his own. He contemns, ridicules, spurns, denounces, or persecutes them; and holds them guilty or contemptible for what he treats as *willful* ignorance and superstition, or evil faith, and for which he, in spirit, if not by actual opposition and persecution, holds them accountable even before the tribunal of his own sentiment and judgment. Perhaps in the same sentence, in which he avows his fatalism or optimism, he contradicts and refutes his own professed sentiment by finding fault with, and denouncing those who oppose his sentiments, or whom he regards as so willfully and criminally ignorant, superstitious, credulous, and perverse as to entertain and promulgate sentiments differing from his own. In every-expression of approbation or disapprobation of human conduct or human sentiment and character, the fatalist acknowledges the freedom of the human mind to will and to act for itself, and its responsibility for its exercise of that freedom.

Indeed, there is in mankind a universal SENSE of freedom of the 'Will, which no influence of the father of lies with man's own efforts. Conjoined, can possibly eradicate. A sense of this freedom is brought into the world with us: it accompanies us through life: and it will -attend the soul eternally. A reasonable and candid mind can require nothing further than this universal sensation, as proof, to demonstration, that the human soul is free to will and to act as it wills.

If mankind, by that universal sense which we have just considered, have the witness of their own freedom, in themselves, the witness 'Of Divine testimony, which is still greater, agreed thereto. The giving to mana law, and attaching to its fulfillment or its transgression, reward or punishment, is ·sufficient evidence that the Giver *of* that law regards its subject as possessing an ability and freedom is himself for obeying or disobeying it. To suppose the contrary, were to regard our Maker, either as not knowing .., what is in man, "or tri- fling with both himself and his creature, mocking man's helplessness with requisitions which cannot be perf6rmed and with punishment for not performing impossibilities. : Such is not the God we worship. His knowledge is infinite: he knows well the work of his own bands. His wisdom is infinite: he cannot mistake in the adaptation of his law to his subject. He is good and just: he does not exercise his-superior power in mockery and oppression of his pleasures. He is a God of truth and sincerity-, and of infinite dignity: he does not trifle with man and with his own authority, by enactment of laws not to be obeyed nor enforced. He does not make a machine to be involuntarily, passively moved by an irresistible power or fatal necessity, and? then, in the formality- of a ruler of a free intelligence, utter a moral law for its observance-while yet it must remain a machine and of resistless necessity move on precisely as if no moral law had been pronounced, and much in opposition to the given law! Far from us be such imputations against the character of the Infinite Majesty!

The Holy Scriptures, throughout, are aluminous with divine truth, that man is free to will, and to act as he wills. In noon-day clearness it beams from every page: Pouring conviction of sin upon every transgressor who sincerely comes to the light; and "vindicating the ways of God to man." Every precept -every commandment -ever admonition-every threatening -every denunciation -every expostulation all warning-every entreaty and promise-every record of judgment against the wicked and of rewarding favor of the righteous-every one of these, in unison with the whole of the Record which God has given us of himself, and with all his dealing with mankind, *declares the freedom of the will and of the whole soul;* in opposition to the notion of subjection to fixed decrees and fatal necessity.

In the revelation which he has given us, he draws aside, with his own hand, the curtain of the past, and pours his light upon the present He shows us man, acting from his own free choice; and him- self, as a righteous Governor, dealing with man accordingly. He draws ·aside the curtain of the future, revealing the judgment scene and the retributions of eternity : showing us that the decisions of that day, in fixing the endless destiny of all mankind, are to be made, in true -

righteousness, on the ground that the human soul is free to will and free to act.

By freedom of the will, we mean its *absolute* freedom : its independence of all motives that may address themselves to it : free to reject the stronger, in favor of the weaker, as it is free to yield to the stronger, in opposition to the weaker.

Such is the original and absolute freedom and power of the human will. With such freedom and such ability it is invested by our Author. He holds us responsible for the exercise of all this freedom and ability. In the first instance of human transgression, the will decided in favor of the weaker motive, to the rejection of the stronger. Can it be doubted that the motive to please his Maker, and avoid the dreadful penalty of transgression, was stronger than the opposite motive, the pleasing his wife or the serpent, and the gratification of passion and appetite *1 yet* he yielded to the weaker or the less motive. In offering pardon, sanctification, and eternal life to the sinner, Christ presents a greater motive than the world and sin: yet how large that class to whom our Lord 1ays, "ye will not come unto me that ye might have life." To talk of the soul being free only to yield to whatever may be considered the strongest motive, were as sensible as to talk of the freedom of a piece of metal to be drawn towards a magnet rather than to an opposite substance possessing no attractive influence upon it.

No: the freedom of the human will is something that in its essence· is· independent of everything in the universe. Its Creator made it so. He made it independent, in its absolute action, of his own law, of his own claims, of himself, of all the motives afforded by the promised· or participated rewards of virtue, of all the threatened woes attached to the transgression of his law-yet as man's moral Governor holding him accountable for the exercise of that freedom. The essence· of that freedom, is beyond our conception. We cannot comprehend it ; nor need we, as it is enough for all practical purpose, that we know ourselves to be possessed of the power, and that we know how to. Properly exercise it: It lies far away in the depths of our Creator's wisdom and his power, farther than our menial can reach. It towers in its moral grandeur higher than our apprehensions can climb. The witness of our own hearts and the testimony of our Maker, assure us that we possess that freedom: we feel the attribute within us: But who can define its essence 1 *Could* we view it-could we grasp it within the arms of our own understanding-from what vocabulary could we gather terms for its description 1 But the supposition is vain. Not even the principles of our corporeal life and faculties can we discern to their essence.

Who can conceive, in what consists the essence of corporeal vitality, our animal life 1 we only know that we possess it: we observe some of its operations: we feel its influences: but whose eye has penetrated to its essence and analyzed or ascertained its real properties.

Much less can mind comprehend mind. If the understanding can proceed no further than the threshold of corporeal life, in its researches ink» the structure of that mysterious temple ; how shall it presume to grasp the attributes of the towering soul, to scan and handle, and to demonstrate and define its most god-like qualities?

Or why should it deny the existence of attributes, the essence of which it cannot describe-impiously presuming itself qualified for the comprehension of whatever God has made; and, perhaps, of all that the Infinite himself is! Such is the arrogance of those who assume to themselves justification in denying all they cannot comprehend.

--How wonderful is man!
Distinguished link in being's endless
chain! Midway from nothing to the
Deity!
Dim miniature of great absolute!
An heir of glory! A frail child of dust
A worm! A god! Tremble at myself.
And in myself am lost. At home a
stranger,
Thought wander up and down,
surprised, about,
And wondering on her own. How
reason reels!
0 what a miracle to man is mans-youth.

Some further observations, to be made on
the subject of this article, are of a nature
peculiarly practical. To them, as such, the
reader's particular attention is invited.

As we have before remarked, the will must
ever remain free.-Freedom to will and to act, is
an attribute of the soul, given it in its Creation.
It is an ingredient of the soul's constitution-of
its existence. In its essence it will endure,
while the soul endure. But, though the soul
must be forever *essentially* freer it may be
circumstantially enslaved. It may not be a
paradox, that the soul is so free that it may
enslave itself. Yet, into what depth of
bondages ever it may sink itself, its

responsibility or accountability does not cease. Because its enslavement is its own voluntary act; and means for its full restoration, such as it still has power to accept and improve, are freely offered in the Gospel, during the time of probation. The Great1 Liberator of souls, on one occasion, said to the people, "If ye continue in my word, then are ye my disciples indeed; and ye shall know the truth, and the truth shall make you free." They answered him, "We be Abraham's seed, and were never in bondage to any mm: how sayest thou, ye shall be made free?"

Our Lord replied, "Verily, verily, I say unto you, whosoever committeth sin is the servant of sin." St. Paul has 'the same sentiment: "Know ye not, that to whom ye yield yourselves servants to obey, his servants ye are whom you obey; whether of sin unto death, or of obedience unto righteousness." He exhorts Timothy to a faithful dispensation of the truth, that by "acknowledging" it, the wicked "may recover themselves out of the snare of the devil, who are taken captive by him at his will." The manner, more particularly, in which men fall into bondage is described in Revelation; and in that description it is- shown that they enter into it voluntarily, by their own free choice: "They are without excuse: because when they knew

God they glorified him not as God, neither were thankful, but became vain in their imaginations, and their foolish heart was darkened. Professing themselves to be wise they became fools, and changed the glory of the incorruptible God into an image made like to corruptible man, and *to* birds, and to four-footed beasts and creeping things. Wherefore, God! Also gave them up to uncleanness, through the lusts of their own hearts. And even as they did not like *to* retain God in their knowledge, God gave them over to a reprobate mind."

Our bodily health is sometimes deeply impaired, and our physical constitution Sometimes reduced to a bad condition, by causes which were unobserved at their occurrence and unsuspected when their evil effects have become developed ; more liable is our mental health, and mental constitution, to become impaired by cause unsuspected, or forgotten, or perhaps unseen. 'The laws of bodily health are far more palpable than those of the mental constitution ; hence, causes affecting the corporeal well-being, are more obvious than those affecting the health of the soul. Yet, ask the sick man, burning and to Sing in prostration upon· his couch, what is the cause of his sickness? He tells you it is a fever. But what is a fever1 or what has caused his fever? Perhaps he will be surprised that you ask him such a question. Like thousands, he has never thought of fever's having any cause. He has always regarded it as some causeless thing that occurs as a-mere matter of course. But his fever is indeed only an object of Borne cause. That cause may have been yesterdays, last week's, or last year's improper exposure to damp and chill. He may have inhaled from the atmosphere the miasma that produced it, months possibly years ago.

It may be the effect of an indigestible meal of ye1terday, or last week, or of improper food or drinks habitually received for months or years, whose effects, little noticed at first, have at length resulted in the present severe illness. Certain it is that something has caused the disease. Some evil influence avoidable or unavoidable has, recently, or remotely, caused this malady. And however trifling the cause might be deemed, the effect is deeply calamitous it has prostrated in feebleness and distress, that man of former vigor. And perhaps it will sweep him away from the stage of life to the grave. But he knows not, suspects not, the cause of this calamity, of this debility and pain and danger. And should it terminate mortally; when he has gone to the tomb and the mourners go about the streets, they will say of their departed friend,' *he died of fever'* - unsuspicious as himself while living, that fever 'had a cause, regarding it as a some- thing that is somehow self-caused and occurring as a fatality or matter of course.

Had he not exposed himself to that chill or damp ; had he not inhaled that miasma; nor partook .of that improper aliment; nor subjected his physical system to deleterious habits or influence, he would not have been brought down to that bed of helplessness and pain and languishing.

Now let us contemplate a case of mental disease, of moral debility or helplessness. Here is a man who is not a Christian. He does not believe the truth of Christianity. And he is in the habit of sinful practices. Ask him wherefore heist thus: and he will be likely to tell you, he is unavoidable what he is. He says he would wish to believe in the Christian religion, and even be a Christian. But he avers that he is of necessity what he is: that he cannot help his belief or disbelief: he cannot believe or disbelieve anything and everything he chooses: he believes *as he does,* and how could he believe otherwise. And further, he a ledges that he is surrounded by motives and he must of necessity yield to those which are strongest. Is this person's condition indeed what he declares it to be? And is be responsible for it, or for his continued course of conduct *and* is such a state compatible with the freedom of the human will?

Impart, his situation is probably what he declares it to be: in part, it *is* probably not what he declares it to be. He is responsible for being in. the situation in which he really is. And that condition is perfectly compatible with the freedom of the will. It may be true he *wishes* he were a Christian. But wishing is not *willing*! 'Here is much difference between these. And it is probably true that he. Could not *at once* and *directly,* in his present circumstances, so *will* and t0 exercise the freedom of the mind, as to, at once, become a believer in Christ. In the case of sickness, supposed above. The person burning and tossed with fever and prostrate with debility, wishes he were otherwise. But he has no power to become now, at once.

He had power, however, to avoid that cold and damp; to shun the atmosphere loaded with sickness; to abstain from deleterious aliment and from unhealthy habits. And now that the cause whatever it may be, bas developed itself in the present calamitous condition, although he has not the power to at once divest himself of disease; yet if he have a skillful physician, or an adviser well instructed in the means of recovery-if he will receive the medicine-if he will diligently employ the proffered means, simple as they may appear, and slowly they may effect and carry forward convalescence-if he will persevere in the sure rules of health-he may arise to health md strength-recovered from his sickness, and rescued from threatening death.

So, the morally diseased. He wishes himself free from his skepticism and the dominion of sin, or what he calls the strongest motives. Had he, in former time, properly exercised his mental freedom; had he not done violence to his mental constitution he would not have been in his present state of moral prostration, debility and disease? He has fallen into it by voluntary, willful violence against the faculties of his own soul. '

The causes of his disease may have commenced in his early childhood. Then, perhaps, be began to partake of the fruits whose poison is as permanent and progressive as now to be working the deep moral death which affects him at this remote period. In early youth, perhaps, he surrendered up, one after another, his virtuous principles for the indulgence of vice; yielded his good resolutions to the assaults of temptation; plunged into dissipation to drown his conscience, and studied apologies to still its accusing; and sought the branding iron of error to sear it to insensibility. And finally, as a most effectual means of sinning without fear of God; without the fearful looking for of indignation that is to devour the adversaries of God; he drank in, ns they were presented by some minister of sin, the deadly waters of Infidelity. All this by the free choice, of the soul, by the exercise of the freedom of the will, he chose to exercise it in favor of sin. What wonder that his soul is all diseased-prostrate-helpless!

And yet there is hope for him. He may not be altogether helpless. God hath laid help on one mighty to save. He saves the chief of sinners. He is the soul's Physician. His skill reaches the most extreme case. He can cure the sceptic, the fatalist, the infidel. But he will do *it* by that sinner's consent; by the co-operation of that sinner's own soul, in the exercise of what freedom of mind he has yet remaining. In infinite condescension he brings down his requisitions to the reduced capacity of the moral patient, and adapts his means to the necessities of his case. Unless mercy's day is past with that sinner, he has moral strength to apply to Christ for healing; to desist from those sine which have operated as the causes of his present malady; to receive the remedies prescribed by the heavenly Physician. Christ is ready to give 1tim all the aid he needs in these things. If the sinner, with what strength he yet has, will comply with the Savior's offers, "he will become convalescent-he will live- be will arise in newness of life-of life that has no end. Hence, the sceptic or fatalist is accountable for being in the conditioning which he is, because he came to it by willful ·sin; and he is accountable for remaining in it, because, in so doing, he willfully rejects the aid of the Savior to raise him to life and strength-willfully refrains from the use of such means and measures for recovery as are offered him.

So little are the laws of mind understood, and their operations observed; so remote are full mental developments, or established conditions of mind, from the causes and influences which have produced them; that the individual has in many, perhaps in most cases, no suspicion of .the causes of his present .mental state. And so voluntarily does the individual act in his exposure to those remote influences, and in "the indulgence of the incipient habits of his soul; that what he regards as a state of mind in which he iii fixed by fatal necessity, is only the legitimate product of his own free choice. The soul may act in such a manner to-day, as will fix it to a certain course to-morrow; it may pursue a course this year which will bind it to a certain course or fix it in a certain state, next year-years to come-- through eternity. True, it may not be the individual's designer wish, or even though, that consequences so deeply and permanently evil should result from causes so apparently small or inert, or that those incipient aberrations would conductor a state so deplorable; yet he acted, in these, freely against what he at the moment knew to be right; and the laws of mind, together with the righteous principles oil which God deals with the subjects of his moral government, and the stewards of his manifold mercies, harmonize together in leaving the transgressor *to* reap the fruits of his own doing at--Only so far as his mercy in Christ Jesus comes in with its offers of help, res- cue, and deliverance. That son, who, in opposition to his father's rightful authority and expressed will, push es his little boat out upon the waters of the smoothly-gliding river, may have no intention of going far from shore, nor thought of floating down the stream.- If he hears the roar of the cataract of which his father has warned him, it is so distant, and the current is so gentle or imperceptible, be way deem it perfectly safe to indulge in disobedience to a slight degree. But transgression yesterday emboldens him to further transgression to-day.

He ventures further, and further; the current grows stronger and stronger: the influence of his father's command upon his mind is weakened by every moment's persistence in disobedience, while the propensity to sinful indulgence acquires strength from habit. Finally he resigns himself up to the course of the current, and per- haps falls asleep or is so absorbed in the delirium of pleasure, that be is long unconscious of his progress. But if, he awake, he may find be current so strong as to render his feeble oar incompetent to its resistance...

Will he say that resistless fate has placed him at the mercy of the stream? It is his willful disobedience that bas done it. Bu yet the pitying love and mercies of his parent follow him. A cord is thrown out, to which he may fix his grasp, and finally be drawn safe to shore. And yet, will he say, because his own oar and arm have become incompetent to withstand the current, or because he cannot be drawn to land without his doing so much as to lay hold upon the extended means of deliverance-will he therefore say that his continued progress and his final precipitancy into the abyss of ruin, are inevitable. If such be his obstinacy, how just, bow unavoidably necessary in the nature of things, that he perish! So just in the retributions of God; so inevitable, from the laws of mind and the constitutional freedom of the soul, is the final destruction of those 'Who yield to temptation, persist in transgression, and despise or reject the interposition of Christ, through the time of probation allotted by infinite goodness, wisdom, and justice conjoined. For the Creator will no destroy that work of his own wisdom, the FREEDOM OF THE SOUL.

The same principles obtaining respect to virtuous influences and incipient operations. The cause or causes which have resulted in the present healthy state of an individual's mind, may have occurred so remotely, that he does not even suspect his present condition to be the result of those remote volitions. He may suppose his present principles, feelings and faith to be spontaneous; while in truth they may be the results of voluntary actions, performed days, weeks, months, years, or many years ago-results produced legitimately from those remote actions by the laws of mind, and in accordance with the economy of .divine dispensations. The peculiarly favored state of mind enjoyed to-day may be given in answer to voluntary obedience and prayer occurring weeks or years ago. These principles are rife with most important considerations for those who have the training of children, the instruction of youth-for parents, teachers, and ministers-for every person, who is to be the maker of his own destiny by the free volitions of his own soul.

We know not how to close this article, better than by quotation of the following text, so fully illustrative of the wise adaptations of the dispensations of God, to the constitution given to the human mind; for the equitable and necessary trial of mankind's candidates, during a life of probation, for an unchangeable eternity : "And thou shalt remember all the way which the Lord thy God led thee, these forty years in the wilderness, to humble thee and to prove thee, to know what was itchy heart, whether thou wouldest keep his commandments, or no."

A DISCOURSE ON
THE FREEDOM OF THE WILL

By
RANSOM DUNN

The F. W. Baptist Church, Boston. 1850

PREFACE.

The following discourse was prepared by the request of the Boston Quarterly Meeting, and but for a request for its publication from the same source would never have gone beyond the limits of the congregation before which it was presented. In order to save time and space, quotations have been almost entirely omitted. But although the language, style, and arrangement, and many of the ideas advanced, cannot honestly be charged upon any other; yet the writer would here once for all acknowledge himself indebted to all from whom he could derive any advantage, especially Edwards, Day, Mahan, and Tappan. Believing that something upon this subject is greatly needed in our churches, this, with some hesitancy, is submitted as a kind of substitute for what we need, until a more able pen is employed. That it may be of some little service to the cause of Christ, and to some few at least, of those with whom his life and interest from childhood have been identified is the sincere desire and earnest of the

AUTHOR. Boston, March 1, 1850 FREEDOM OF THE WILL "For unto whomsoever much is given, of him shall be much required: and to whom men have committed much, of him they will ask the more." Luke 12:48.

That human obligation is precisely in proportion to human ability, is the doctrine of this text. This doctrine applied to our relations to the divine government, constitutes one of the distinguishing peculiarities, and is the occasion of the distinguishing name, of that portion of the church with which we are connected. Three questions, however, are necessarily embraced in this subject, and perhaps were contemplated in the resolution requiring this discourse. Is the will free, or necessary, in its volitions? Is the atonement limited or unlimited, in its provisions for man? Is election to eternal life conditional or unconditional? Are all necessarily embraced in the subject of free salvation? The discussion of them all in one discourse would be impossible. I have therefore concluded to confine myself to the first. And the consideration, even of this topic, within the narrow limits assigned, will be attended with serious difficulties. To avoid these difficulties, technical and philosophical terms must be avoided as far as possible, and such terms, arguments, and illustrations used as will require the least possible explanation. This course is the more readily adopted in view of the fact, that a last portion of the field from which the arguments and illustrations upon this subject are drawn, is open to all, and accessible by persons of every degree of ability. The supposition that this subject is so philosophical and metaphysical, as to be above the common mind, is altogether a mistake. Whether our volition are free or necessary, is a question to be settled wholly by the development of the mind itself; and therefore, every individual possesses the volume from which he may read the truth, and the whole truth, upon this subject. Two positions have been taken respecting volition and the will.

Some have contended that every volition, choice, or determination, was the effect of motive, and that motive invariably sustained the relation of cause, and of necessary causes, to all acts of the will. And, that, in every cause the existence of the antecedent (motive,) renders the sequent, (volition,) necessary, and necessarily just what it is.

Others contend that whatever relation motive may sustain to volition, it is not that of necessary cause. If motive be an antecedent, it is one from which either of two or more sequents may follow. It is also believed by this cause of Metaphysicians and Theologians, that motive is not the cause of volition, unless by motive is understood the power that determines. And that notwithstanding motive is always present in volition, yet it is the object acted upon and not the agent that moves the mind. And that man is free in this sense-that at any given time his volitions are so caused, by the causative principle in his own mind, that they might not have been, or that they might have been different from what they are.

This is the doctrine of this discourse. And in its discussion, it is my design:

I. To answer some of the objections urged against the freedom of the Will.

II. Present some arguments for its support.

III. Give a brief summary of objections to the doctrine of necessity.

Let us proceed then,

I. Answers To Some Of The Objections Which Are Brought Against The Position Assumed In This Discourse.

1. The Metaphysician affirms that everything is either necessary or contingent. If volition is not necessary, then it is contingent; and if contingent, then it occurs by mere chance; and is as liable to be in one direction as in another, regardless of all influences and motives. But every effect must have a cause; volition is an effect, and therefore must have a cause. If everything is necessary or contingent, and if contingency implies the absence of all cause, then it follows necessarily, if volition be an effect, it must be necessary, and necessarily just as it is. This is almost the entire burden of President Day's work on the Will. In reply, it may be said, that contingency is not here properly explained. It is not used in opposition to cause, but in opposition to necessity. The question is not whether volition is uncaused, but whether the relation of motive to volition is that of necessary cause. To affirm that

everything contingent is without cause, is to destroy all idea of contingency. Everything is caused but the Deity, and His existence is certainly necessary, therefore nothing, upon this hypothesis, can be contingent. If there may be events, rendered contingent by the possibility of either of two or more results from their causes, which we know is possible, then this objection is groundless.

2. But the Logician applies a part of this objection in a different manner. If every effect must have an adequate cause, and if volition be an effect, then every volition must have an antecedent. And hence all choice depends upon pre-existing motive, and the greatest motive, or, "greatest apparent good," is the cause of every particular volition. This is the sum and substance of Edwards' celebrated "Inquiry on the Will."

(1.) Here again, we have the erroneous assumption, that antecedents and causality, imply necessity. It is simply saying, that because volitions take place, (for they must be effects,) therefore they cannot be free, or contingent. It is begging, or at least overlooking, the entire question in dispute.

(2.) The affirmation, that the greatest motive invariably governs, is a mere assumption, incapable of proof. We ask, how does anyone know that he is governed by the greatest motive? The answer, and the only answer possible, is, that he is thus influenced. But, how does he know that he is thus influenced? Because the greatest motive governs. And thus the assumption is the proof, and the proof the assumption, and finally they are both assumptions, incapable of any proof. This is reasoning in a circle with a short curve. It is simply saying that we know how man is influenced, because we know the nature of the cause; and we know the nature of the cause, because we know how he is influenced.

(3.) This idea of cause and effect, antecedents and sequences, as thus applied, would necessarily imply an eternal succession of antecedents, which is an absurdity. If the volition we now form is caused by a pre-existing motive, that motive must also have had a cause, and its cause must also have been produced, and thus you may proceed ad infinitum. It is saying there is a succession of periods, every one of which had a beginning, and yet one did not begin. A chain of events, every one of which must have been caused, and yet one (the first) could not have been caused. And if the objector sees fit to hang the chain upon the volition of God, he is not at all relieved. For I remark:

(4.) We are not reasoning upon this subject merely in reference to the phenomena of the human will. The objection refers to volitions and their antecedents, irrespective of the being in which such volitions take place. Now, if every volition implies an antecedent motive, in view of which the volition is formed, and formed necessarily just as it is; then, either God wills without motive, or else he not only wills in view of motive, but is in each respective volition governed by a previously existing motive. And, therefore, this difficulty is only rendered more difficult by referring it to the Deity.

3. But the Theologian urges the foreknowledge of God as an objection to our position. What God foreknows will come to pass, must necessarily take place; is the universal objection of all necessitarians, to moral freedom.

(1.) We know of no mode of knowledge which implies causality. The simple perception or consciousness of an act or event, is in every mind clearly distinct from the cause or power which produces it. Therefore, whatever degree of certainty may be affirmed of any event upon the ground of knowledge, its cause must be looked for somewhere else. If

God knows things upon principles entirely different from any with which man is acquainted, our ignorance of the mode of such knowledge renders the objection groundless.

(2.) But if our knowledge of future events is analogous to His, divine foreknowledge can have nothing to do with causality. The Astronomer makes his calculations respecting the motions and changes of the planets for years to come, and with mathematical certainty knows and states his conclusions; and yet who believes that his knowledge has anything to do with the causality or necessity of such events? And does any knowledge we have of the future differ from this in this respect? It may be said, that much if not most of our knowledge of the future depends upon the knowledge of causes which render the events certain. This is true, but still everyone knows that the knowledge is not the cause, nor the cause the knowledge; but that they are perfectly distinct. Every child who knows enough to know that if he thrusts his hand into the fire, it will be burned, knows too that his knowledge of the fact is not the fire, nor the power that produces the heat. But if foreknowledge when applied to the divine character, does not mean the same as when applied to human character, then what does it mean, but present knowledge?

(3.) God's foreknowledge is not of the same nature with our forecast. All knowledge is necessarily of two kinds. It is mediate or immediate, viz., we know by direct perception or consciousness, or else through the medium of an object or evidence, which lies between us and the object or fact known; e. g., I know there is such a place as Canton; but, do not know it by direct perception. I know there is such a place as Boston, upon a different principle. The future or foreknowledge of the astronomer is through an intermediate object or evidence, and is inferential. He knows the event because he knows its cause. But his knowledge of the planet upon which he is now gazing does not thus depend upon previous knowledge or evidence. He knows its present position and aspect because he sees it regardless of all causes.

If God is infinite, filling all space, and even filling all duration, there, can be no object or evidence between him and the object or fact known. All knowledge, therefore, with him must be immediate and direct. He does not know an event because something else is known, or because of the knowledge of some antecedent cause; but by direct perception. And all events, whether caused by his own power or the agency of others, are known, not in consequence of necessary cause, but simply because they occur. Things are known, not because they must be, but because they are. And in knowing our volitions, he knows them as our volitions; and because they are put forth, and not because they are made certain by his determinations or decrees.

Again, it should be remembered that all knowledge is present knowledge. The fore and after, which we apply to knowledge, have reference to the object of knowledge, not the knowledge. If we know of an event that occurred yesterday, we know it now. Memory brings up the event now, and makes it a present knowledge. If we possessed the power of prescience, sustaining the same relation to the future that memory does to the past, the knowledge would be present, and the one would have as little to do with the causality or necessity of events as the other. God's foreknowledge, then, although it makes it certain that an event does occur, no more makes it certain that such an event might not have been otherwise, than my knowledge of your presence here today makes it certain that you could not have been elsewhere. You could have been elsewhere, and then the knowledge of your position would have been accordingly. Our actions might have been different from what they are, and God's knowledge would have been according to the facts in the case.

The idea that simple knowledge implies necessity with respect to cause, is not according to sound philosophy, common sense, nor the Bible.

II. Some Positive Arguments In Support Of The Doctrine Of "Free-Will."

1. We will listen to the voice of consciousness. By consciousness is here understood, not the power which knows, but the recognizing of the knowledge. It is that field upon which the mind, on the one hand, and the external world, on the other meets. We are not conscious of anything with- out the mind; but in perceiving objects, sensations are produced of which we are conscious. We are not conscious even of the powers of mind, as such, but these powers produce sensations of which we are conscious. This field of sensation or consciousness, then, is the ground of all oar knowledge. No external object is known unless there exists such a correlation between the object and the mind as to produce sensation. And no power of mind is known except by its action, which produces sensation. It is evident, therefore, that our knowledge of the mind, and especially of the will, must be derived from this source.

If we investigate this field, I think we shall perceive that the sensations from objects without, and the mind within, clearly indicate the possibility of our volitions, at any given time, being different from what they are and that it is only upon this principle that we have any idea of right and wrong in character, or of praise-worthiness or blame-worthiness, in ourselves or others.

But there are some general developments of common consciousness upon this subject.

(1.) Language comprises but signs of ideas; and any term or form of expression, supposes the pre-existence of the idea expressed. In every language and tongue spoken, there are words and phrases, implying the freedom of the will. Thus said, "We ought not to have done thus," or "We ought to have determined upon a different course," viz. If necessitarianism be true, we ought not to have complied with an eternal immutable, divine law, which God himself could not have broken; or we ought to have violated such a law. So when we express regret or astonishment that volitions in ourselves or others should have been as they are, we use language unmeaning, nonsensical, and sinful, if they, were determined by the Almighty, and could not have been otherwise.

The same is true of all language used in expostulation, or threatening or even commanding.

(2.) Not only the language, but the laws of all nations, civilized or barbarous, indicate most conclusively the decision of consciousness upon this subject. Do they not all proceed upon the supposition that when a subject determines to do right, he might have determined to do wrong, and that when he determines to do wrong he might have determined to do right.

(3.) And, does not the justification or condemnation others show most conclusively, the position of consciousness upon this question?

The disposition to justify and condemn seems to arise instinctively, as from a principle of our natures. Even before language is learned, the infant mind develops this disposition. And just in proportion as mind is developed, distinctions are made between the intelligent and unintelligent portions of creation, and praise or blame awarded to the former and none to the latter. Why this disposition, and why this distinction between voluntary and material agency, if all things, and all things alike, are governed by the same unalterable laws of necessity? And why has God thus made one portion of creation to oppose and find fault with another, if the same necessity governs the action and tendency of both?

2. Notwithstanding this is purely a psychological subject, and should be treated as such, yet there are certain necessary logical deductions arising from the two systems now under consideration, which will aid us materially in deciding upon their respective merits.

What are the necessary consequences of necessitarianism?

If volition is necessitated, and can in no given case be different from what it is, then there can be no responsibility attending volition. If we cannot hold the knife responsible for stabbing a man, while the hand which grasps the knife and directs the blow is held by another, how can we hold the man responsible while the power which constitutes his agency is held and controlled by force beyond his agency? We hold a man responsible for presenting motives even when they do not prevail. Where, then, does responsibility rest when in every case, and necessarily in every case, volition is as the motive?--upon our actions, here effects, or upon the actual cause of that action, the author of the motive?

It has been said that responsibility rests upon natural, not moral ability. But Edwards himself tells us that the difference between natural and moral ability does not consist in the nature of the necessity, but simply in the terms thus related. Moral necessity referring to volitions and their cause, motives; and natural necessity, to the connection between physical causes and their effects. Natural and moral ability and inability differ then only in the same way. Natural inability, is inability to do what we will; moral inability, an inability to will. There is no difference in the necessity. The one is as fatal as the other, and implies as little responsibility. Now, either. There is, or there is not any occasion for this distinction between natural and moral ability. If there is not such occasion, and if volition is necessary, then the same fatal necessity pervades alike the whole universe; and there is as much responsibility resting upon the physical as the moral world. But, if there is an occasion for such distinction, then, to base moral obligation upon natural or physical ability, is as inconsistent as to require a man naturally blind to see, because, forsooth, he could hear- or to require a man to move an arm which he never possessed, because he has a foot. If a man is not the cause of his own volitions, and in that sense possessed of moral ability, he cannot be responsible. Moral responsibility cannot rest upon natural ability.

But again, motive is unintelligent and irresponsible; and, therefore, the Author of motive is the only being in the universe who is responsible; and he is responsible for every action. But if He determines our volitions, He thus determines in view of motive. For upon the hypothesis now before us, a volition in the Eternal Mind, without an antecedent motive, would be just as impossible as in our own. Therefore there never was a divine volition without a pre-existing motive. Hence there was a time when there was no force in the universe, but the force of motive; and when there either was no God, or else no active God. If we take one horn of the dilemma, and say there was a God, but a God without volition, and consequently without activity or character, we have the Pantheist's God. If we take the other, and affirm that previous to volition there was no intelligent God, we have the God of the Atheist. In either case, the universe presents but a vast blind machine, driven by fate through the immensity, of space and duration.

Attending these necessary results, there are several inferences which might be drawn; but one of which, however, can with due regard to our assigned limits, be here admitted.

If the above mentioned hypothesis and its necessary consequences be correct, then all distinctions between good and evil are hypothetical and imaginary. Both are in compliance with fixed, immutable law. Hence all distinctions between vice and virtue, and all restraints or encouragements, family, civil or religious, growing out of these distinctions, are false and vain.

But what are the deductions from the supposition that the will is self-determining? At all events, the difficulties cannot be greater, the consequences more absurd, than those which arise from the opposite system. It cannot be an absurdity, for the practice of all men, in all the common affairs of life, has been based upon this freedom, and common consciousness and spontaneous convictions have always sustained this doctrine.

Upon the supposition of its truth, man at once appears an accountable being; he himself, and no other one, being responsible for his volitions. He is thus rendered a fit subject of moral government. The institution of human governments, and the organization of the family, with all the voluntary relations and influences growing out of them, are thus made legitimate and reasonable. Language and the plainest decisions of consciousness, which would otherwise present the most inexplicable difficulties, are thus rendered plain and simple. The atonement, with all the means of grace, the disciplinary influences of providence, and all human efforts for the change of character, which would otherwise be but a solemn farce, at once appear necessary and consistent.

3. But the practical influences of the two systems must not be passed over.

It will not be assumed that all believers in necessitarianism are wicked men, nor that all believers in moral freedom are good. There are many exceptions upon both sides, and many whose character is not materially affected by any particular views entertained respecting this question. But still, it seems to me, that there are certain facts connected with this aspect of the subject, which deserve our serious consideration. And,

(1st.) Invariably, those who have denied human responsibility and accountability, have based that denial upon the doctrine of necessity. But who ever heard of an individual believing in the freedom of the will, as above explained, who denied man's accountability? Such an instance never was known.

(2d.) Almost all of the greatest errors in religion and morals, have been advocated upon the ground of moral necessity, and many of them based exclusively upon this theory.

This is the beginning and the end with the Atheist. It is the sum total of the Pantheist's scheme. And the Deist, Universalist, Fatalist and Antinomian, in defending their respective systems, are equally dependent upon the supposition, that whatever is, is so of necessity; and that therefore whatever is, is right. When we reflect, that the doctrine we are now controverting is not an incidental item in these systems, but one of the fundamental assumptions upon which their advocates all base them, and that they are not defended without this assumption, are we not forced to the conclusion that in its practical result there is a refutation of all claims to truth; unless indeed, these systems be true. But has the doctrine of freedom ever been used for any such purpose? If so, I am not aware of the fact.

(3.) And is it not an undeniable fact, that the most immoral and irreligious, are generally warm advocates of the doctrine of necessity; and especially when pressed upon moral or religious obligations. I know it is said, they only fly to this for a refuge. But this is making a great admission, namely, that the system constitutes a very convenient garb for such characters. Can a doctrine so peculiarly adapted to such a work, and so generally associated with such characters, be true, even though many of the best men of the world have believed it?

But do men ever apologize for their crimes upon the ground that they are free agents, capable of choosing a different course, and responsible for not doing so?

(4.) Another significant fact which bears upon this subject, is seen in the course pursued by the best classes of those opposed to our position.

Is it not universally known, that in their efforts for changing the hearts and characters of men--for promoting morality and religion, they leave entirely out of sight their peculiar views upon this question, and address themselves to common sense and common consciousness.

Does the moralist in his efforts to reform the blasphemer or nebriate, begin with an essay upon moral necessity, and after convincing his disciples that his volitions could not have been different from what they are, and that any change in his future course depends exclusively upon motives beyond his control, and that such motives win as certainly control him as the unobstructed weight falls to the earth, proceed to urge a change of life? None labor in his way. And to pursue such a course would exhibit as little claim to sanity, as an effort to persuade the Mississippi to just roll back from its mouth over the falls of St. Anthony.

And what is the course of the pastor when laboring with an impenitent sinner, or in a season of special religious interest in his congregation? Is not the instruction and preaching at such times so emphatically "free-will" that the most sectarian "Free-willer" is perfectly satisfied?

Does not this fact go to show most conclusively, that our opponents themselves have no confidence in the practical influence of their doctrine, and especially when any great practical interest is at stake? The facts that convicted men generally urge this doctrine as an apology, for impenitence, and that nine-tenths of all who fall into final religious despair, do so through its influence, and other circumstances indicating its practical influence we have not room for discussing.

4. But the belief that any such power as will is possessed by man is to my mind an evidence of its freedom.

As above remarked, we know of no powers of mind but by their action. If volition is but a necessary sequence of an antecedent correlation between intelligent sensibility and an external object, then nothing more is brought into action than intelligence and sensibility. This phenomenon is to be accounted for, by supposing the existence of these powers, but no other. As well might a man suppose that because he feels a sensation from the fingers of his hand, that therefore, he has one upon the back of his hand; or that because he has eyes, that therefore he must possess some other organs differing entirely from these, as to suppose that because he is conscious of phenomena resulting from reason and sensitivity, that therefore he has a will. I know that consciousness will here be appealed to, and we shall be told that every man knows that he has a will. This is admitted and this is the strength of the argument. Man knows he has a will. But he must know this by phenomena arising directly from such a faculty, differing from that arising from the sensibility or reason.

If volition be necessary, it is but the action of the sensibility, and can in no sense be any evidence of the existence of any other faculty.

This argument is presented with the more confidence, in view of the fact that Edwards makes no distinction between the will and sensibility. He refers to but two grand divisions of the mind; the knowing and the attractive powers. Under this last division, he classes desires, in affections, volitions and every other development of will or sensibility- and then makes volition a result from relation between an object and these powers, thus tacitly admitting that his theory virtually destroys all distinct idea of the will and makes it sensitivity, or mental attraction, If any man can show how he knows that he has a will by such sensations, let him attempt it. And if the universal belief that such a power is possessed does not result from phenomena which can result only from the freedom of the will, I know not where it could have originated!

5. But the last class of argument, to which I refer, is drawn from the Scriptures. But here it

may be observed, the Bible is not given for a scientific text book, nor for a system of philosophy. Those natural common matters of fact with which we are able to become acquainted by other means, are there taken for granted.

That man has some knowledge is everywhere assumed. The word of God nowhere tells us the number or uses of the senses. Neither does it teach mental philosophy, nor directly discuss the subject now under consideration. Mental or psychological facts must be proved from the Bible just as we should prove the existence or use of the senses, or any other physical fact. We must prove the freedom of the will just as we should prove its existence. Were we to attempt either, we should inquire, what does the Bible everywhere assume respecting this subject? Do references to individuals and special circumstances throw any light upon it? What, respecting the question is implied in the doctrines of Christianity?

If then, we throw an eye upon the general surface of the sacred page, and look at its history and laws, its promises and threatening, its revelations and prophecies does not every reference to human nature or character assume the freedom of the will? Nothing is more clearly assumed than this.

And if we look at specific references to times, persons, and events, do we not see the same assumption? Do not all these references to times of prosperity or adversity, to individuals or nations, to events, providential or human, imply the freedom of the will?

Pharaoh, Jacob, and a few others, have been suggested as exceptions. These subjects more properly belong to the questions respecting election and the atonement. And, therefore, without pausing to give specific explanations respecting the texts referred to, it may be said:

(1.) That these are isolated cases. Providing that unusual and even compulsory influences were in these few instances exerted, it would no more prove the general necessity of volition, than miracles prove that God can work in no other way.

(2.) These cases have nothing to do with specific purposes, or personal character. They refer to general positions, of nations or individuals, and have no more to do with the liberty or necessity of the will, than a residence in Europe or America.

But what is implied in the doctrines of the

Bible. Take for instance the fall of man. How did Adam fall? He yielded to the greatest motive, "the greatest apparent good," says the Calvinist. Then, one of two things must have been true. Either there actually was more "good" connected with sin than holiness; or else his mind, as it came from God, was so constituted that it was more easily influenced in that direction than the other. Let him take which horn of the dilemma he may, the conclusion is inevitable, that God intended, determined, and directly caused that event, and all the guilt and misery arising there from. But the fall of man implies no such thing. He was free, not as the water to run downhill, but free to choose or refuse the motives presented.

And respecting the atonement. Why is it given and adapted to man, and not to other portions of creation, if all are governed by the same law of necessity? How can we account for the change which is there contemplated in man's character, circumstances and prospects, if his will is not free? Indeed, God cannot contemplate any change, by an atonement or otherwise, in man's character or relations without a change in himself, unless man is capable of causing a change in himself. Hence the doctrines of pardon and regeneration, as well as the doctrine of atonement, implies the truth of our position. So does every doctrine of the Bible.

But we can notice but one more. Look at the judgement. What of all the warnings and appeals in view of it, what of all the solemn attending circumstances, and what of the judgment itself, if man is to be judged upon the same principle with matter? And what shall we think of the character of the judge, if he is not judged upon the same principle, if he is here governed upon the same principle? And here let it be remembered that the advocates of the doctrine of necessary volition do not claim that there is any difference between moral and physical necessity in the nature of the relation. They affirm that the necessity is precisely the same, and that the terms refer to the objects related, and not to the degree or nature of the necessity. How, if this be true, could God be just and judge the world? If man's volitions and actions are all, invariably and necessarily, governed by motives which God himself controls, how, while sentence is pronounced against a sinner, could the angels sing, "Holy, holy, holy, Lord God Almighty?" Could the inhabitants of heaven say, "Alleluia," while the wicked are "driven away in their wickedness," "and the smoke of their torment ascendeth up for ever and ever." Can we force the hand of a child into the flames, and then punish him for his folly? Can the universe say,

Amen, to the judgments of God, if he forces our volitions, by overpowering motives, and then punishes for these volitions? The judgment in every aspect most clearly implies that man's volitions are as much his own as his actions, and that he is at liberty in his volitions to such an extent, that he is not only the cause of them, but at any given time they might be different from what they are. Indeed, it seems to me impossible that any, man could ever reconcile the doctrine of a judgment with the doctrine of necessity; and I do not wonder that many believers in the latter doctrine have denied the former. Having endeavored to answer some of the most prominent objections against the freedom of the will, and presented a few of the many arguments in favor of this important doctrine, let us conclude:

III. A Brief Summary And Repetition Of Our Objections To The Opposite System.

1. It makes God a tyrant. He requires one thing and then, with a fatal moral necessity, impels man in an opposite direction, and then punishes him for not acting contrary to the "greatest apparent good," which is a work that God himself, even, as our opponents affirm, cannot do.

2. It makes God contradict himself. He

commands one thing, and then with another will, (for it cannot be the same,) absolutely, by moral force, effects their violation.

3. It makes even God a being of necessity, and dependent for his being or capability of action, upon something prior to himself.

4. It makes him the author of all sin. No sin, is committed according to this theory, but in accordance with the greatest motive; and he governs these motives. This is especially true in the case of our first parents, and of the fallen angels. Taking the cause of their transgression out of themselves, it necessarily leaves it in God.

5. It destroys all idea of probation. What idea of trial can be attached to a class of beings who have no control over themselves, or to a state where every action is necessarily as it is, and could not have been otherwise?

6. It destroys all human responsibility. All who deny accountability do so upon this ground; and a large proportion of those who attempt to apologize for neglect of known duty, urge the same plea.

7. It destroys all distinction between vice and virtue. The one is as necessary and

undeniable, and as much in accordance with God's will, as the other.

8. It is the principal ingredient in some of the worst errors which ever cursed the earth.

9. It mystifies the gospel, rendering it contradictory; and thus produces skepticism. Who ever heard of a man turning from religions views or influences, to infidelity, without first embracing necessitarianism?

10. It frequently produces despair in anxious minds; and in this way is the cause of a total neglect of the gospel, or, what is more common, an apology for impenitence.

11. It is generally believed by the worst of men, and made an apology for their crimes.

12. It is not congenial with the spirit of reform, of revivals, and of deep piety. Any of its advocates are reformers, revivalists, and deeply pious men. But, in their efforts for reforms and revivals, and in their most devotional exercises, they act as though they could act, and forget all necessity back of the will.

Brethren, we love reform. We wish to see the wicked forsake his way, and the unrighteous man his thoughts. We wish to see the inebriate restored, and the slave set at liberty. We love the spirit of revival. We wish to see the open gates of Zion thronged with anxious inquirers, saying "what shall we do to be saved." As we feel for these interests and sympathize with suffering humanity, and as we long for the salvation of deathless souls, let us urge the claims of God upon man's free-will. Standing still under the banner of Christ as unfurled by our revered fathers in the gospel, let us walk worthy of the name whereby we have been called; and cheerfully discharge those obligations for the neglect of which we acknowledge ourselves without excuse.

Freedom Of The Will

www.ingramcontent.com/pod-product-compliance
Lightning Source LLC
Chambersburg PA
CBHW060701030426
42337CB00017B/2709